How to Get Free Government Grants

A Step by Step Guide to Getting Free Money From the Government

MEIR LIRAZ

Published by BizMove
www.bizmove.com

Table of Contents

MEIR LIRAZ

1. Here's What's Available to You Courtesy of The US Government

Each day over one million Dollars in free government grants is given away to people just like you for a wide variety of business and personal needs

In this guide I'll tell you exactly HOW & WHERE to get grants. This money has to be given away, WHY not to YOU?

You may be thinking, "How can I get some of this Free Grants Money"

Maybe you think it's impossible to get free money?

Let me tell you it's not impossible! It's a fact, ordinary people and businesses all across the United States are receiving millions of dollars from these Government and Private Foundation's every day.

Who can apply?

ANYONE can apply for a Grant from 18 years old and up!

Grants from $500.00 to $50,000.00 are possible! GRANTS don't have to be paid back, EVER! Claim your slice of the FREE American Pie.

This money is not a loan, Trying to get money through a conventional bank can be very time consuming and requires a lot of paperwork, only to find out that you've been denied. These Government Agencies don't have to operate under the same stringent requirements that banks do.

You decide how much money you need, as long as it's a lawful amount and meets with the Government Agencies criteria, the money is yours to keep and never has to be repaid. This money is non taxable & interest free.

None of these programs require a credit check, collateral, security deposits or co-signers, you can apply even if you have a bankruptcy or bad credit, it doesn't matter, you as a tax payer and U.S. citizen are entitled to this money.

There are currently over 2,000 Federal Programs, 24,000 State Programs, 30,000 Private Foundations and 20,000 Scholarship Programs available.

This year over $30 Billion Dollars In Free Government Grants Money will be given away by Government Grants Agencies.

With an economy that remains unpredictable, and a need for even greater economic development on all fronts, the federal government is more willing than it ever has been before to give you the money you need to.

In spite of the perception that people should not look to the government for help, the great government give-away programs have remained so incredibly huge.

Most people never apply for a free grant because they

somehow feel it isn't for them, feel there's too much red-tape, or simply don't know who to contact. The fact is, however, that people from all walks of life do receive free grant money and other benefits from the government, and you should also.

How to Find funding Sources Worth Billions

As with all grant seeking, the key to obtaining grants is preparation and a knowledge about funding sources. Preparation means identifying programs that are available, and then determining if you fall within their restrictions.

This book will point you to sources that will be invaluable to you in locating thousands of sources of free money!

As you contact different agencies for grant money, learn not to accept "no" as a final answer. There are so many new programs being offered each year that often an agency's own employees won't be aware they are offering the one you ask about. If being persistent doesn't help, get in touch with your congressman and let them track down a program that meets your needs.

2. How to Apply For a Government Grant

To write a successful grant application for free money it should be well planned. You should be familiar with exactly how a particular agency prefers to have their grant proposals completed.

Once you decide which government agency you want free money from, contact them and ask for a grant application kit. Get to know some of the grantor agency personnel. Experts love to talk about their programs, so ask for advice, suggestions, and criticisms about your proposed project.

In most cases, the more an agency knows about your grant proposal, the better your chances will be of getting support from the personnel who ultimately approve your free money request.

Often it is a grantor's advantage to send their grant proposal summary to an agency official they have developed a contact relationship with, and ask them to review and return it to you with their comments. Be certain this approach is acceptable with your agency contact. You wouldn't want a first draft mistakenly processed before it was finished.

Making a personal visit to the agency's office in your area is also important. Face to face contact will help you understand eligibility requirements, deadlines, maximum free money amounts you can apply for, and other details you want to know about. You can also utilize an agency's library and determine through books, brochures, and conversation if there are other agencies you could apply to for free money. There is nothing that says you can't apply for two, three, or more free money grants at one time!

Do some networking and maintain continuous contact with people who can gather information for you about free money grants. Nothing can be substituted for personal contact with the decision makers who are in charge of grant programs. Learn to use your personal influence (and theirs) to achieve your goals.

Applying for government grants: step by step guidelines

1. Browse the sources presented in this book to locate grant programs which are suitable to your needs as an applicant.

2. Determine a means of approach for making an application by considering:

Program Objectives and Uses

Type of Assistance Needed

Eligibility Requirements

Application Procedure Required

3. Check for an application deadline.

4. Refer to the *Information Contacts* section located within each program description for addresses and telephone numbers to obtain further information from the funding agency.

5. Contact the agency to determine:

Applicability of your proposal or project.

Availability of funds or assistance.

Answers to any questions you may have.

6. Apply to the funding agency for assistance. See below for help regarding writing grant proposals.

Tips for Applying for Federal Grants

Continuously seek grant opportunities.

Keep ongoing contact with organizations that award grants.

Decide who will receive information on grants, who will write the proposals and who will manage the grants.

Plan how the grant will be integrated into your overall plans.

Read carefully and follow the application directions.

Be specific and concise with information in the grant application.

Grant applications must be easy to read.

- Each section of the application should relate to the others to create a fluid document.

- Write short paragraphs.

- Provide headings for different sections.

Grant must be properly and professionally written.

- Include a cover letter.

- Provide an introduction with a summary of the proposal.

- Provide a table of contents if the grant is lengthy or broken into sections.

- Give reason for the need of the grant. Identify the problem to be addressed then narrow the focus to the precise use of the grant.

- Provide long and short term objectives.

- Present the standards for the program. What is the target for success and how will it be measured

- Give a future for the program once the grant is complete.

- Include a budget; specify administrative and program costs.

Be complete; try to allow time for review.

- Providing a high quality document, addressing all key elements will increase success.

- Check if grant needs to be reviewed locally under

Executive Order 12372.

Get support from elected officials, business leaders and community leaders.

Follow all grant proposal submittal requirements. These can vary for each grant.

Do not miss deadlines.

Government Grant Application Forms

You need to read the requirements for the program(s) you are interested in. While some programs have their own specific application forms, many use the following for applications.

Standard Form 424, Application for Federal Assistance:

http://www.nist.gov/recovery/upload/SF424.pdf

3. Here's How to Locate a Grant That Fits Your Specific Needs and Situation

The best way to locate government benefits that fit your needs and wants is to use the following online tool. Once you answer all the required questions it will provide you with a list of government benefits that you are qualified for. Access this tool here:

http://www.benefits.gov/benefits/benefit-finder#benefits&qc=cat_1

Here's another useful tool for locating free government money sources. The following online catalog describes all federal government grant and assistance programs - including grants for personal needs (a total of more than 2000 programs). It contains information on all financial and non-financial assistance programs administered by the departments and establishments of the Federal government. Use the search feature to look for areas that interest you:

Go to the following page online to access the list of programs:

https://cfda.symplicity.com/index?s=program&mode=list&tab=list

Once you located one or more benefits that you are interested in and are qualified for, write down their Funding Opportunity Numbers (FON), you'll need it for the next step, the application submission.

4. How To Locate a Grant or a Loan for Starting or Expanding a Business

To locate grants, loans and assistant programs for starting a new business or expanding an existing one, follow these steps:

1. Browse thru the Complete list of all US government grant programs for business grants:

https://cfda.symplicity.com/index?&s=program&mode=list&tab=list&tabmode=list

2. Contact your local SBA office to see what grant and loan programs are available. Click on the link below to locate your local SBA office:

http://www.sba.gov/localresources/index.html

3. Contact your state's Small Business Development Center and find out what programs are available. Go to this online page to locate your local SBDC office:

https://www.sba.gov/tools/local-assistance/sbdc

4. See if you are eligible for a low interest loan from the small Business Administration:

https://www.sba.gov/loans-grants/see-what-sba-offers/sba-loan-programs

5. Get a personal free expert advice and counseling:

You can get personal free expert advice and counseling, in your area, through a volunteer organization called SCORE. The Service Corps of Retired Executives Association (SCORE), is a locally-chartered volunteer organization sponsored by the US Small Business Administration, which provides free expert problem-solving assistance to small businesses. Helping American small businesses to prosper has been SCORE's goal since the program began in 1964.

SCORE tries to match counselor experience with client needs and provide one-to-one counseling. SCORE also conducts well-developed pre-business workshops and a variety of business oriented seminars and training sessions.

To find your nearest SCORE Office, call, nationwide toll-free, National SCORE Office: 1-800-634-0245 or call

SBA: 1-800-U-ASK-SBA

Visit SCORE Association Website:

https://www.score.org/

5. How to Write a Successful Grant Proposal

(Note that this chapter is more applicable for a community or an organization seeking government funding rather than an individual)

Preparation

A successful grant proposal is one that is well-prepared, thoughtfully planned, and concisely packaged. The potential applicant should become familiar with all of the pertinent program criteria related to the Catalog program from which assistance is sought. Refer to the information contact person listed in the Catalog program description before developing a proposal to obtain information such as whether funding is available, when applicable deadlines occur, and the process used by the grantor agency for accepting applications. Applicants should remember that the basic requirements, application forms, information and procedures vary with the Federal agency making the grant award.

Individuals without prior grant proposal writing experience may find it useful to attend a grantsmanship workshop. A workshop can amplify the basic information presented here. Applicants interested in additional readings on grantsmanship and proposal development should consult the references listed at the end of this section and explore other library resources.

INITIAL PROPOSAL DEVELOPMENT

Developing Ideas for the Proposal

When developing an idea for a proposal it is important to determine if the idea has been considered in the applicant's locality or State. A careful check should be made with legislators and area government agencies and related public and private agencies which may currently have grant awards or contracts to do similar work. If a similar program already exists, the applicant may need to reconsider submitting the proposed project, particularly if duplication of effort is perceived. If significant differences or improvements in the proposed project's goals can be clearly established, it may be worthwhile to pursue Federal assistance.

Community Support

Community support for most proposals is essential. Once proposal summary is developed, look for individuals or groups representing academic, political, professional, and lay organizations which may be willing to support the proposal in writing. The type and caliber of community support is critical in the initial and subsequent review phases. Numerous letters of support can be persuasive to a grantor agency. Do not overlook support from local government agencies and public officials. Letters of endorsement detailing exact areas of project sanction and commitment are often requested as part of a proposal to a Federal agency. Several months may be required to develop letters of endorsement since something of value (e.g., buildings, staff, services) is sometimes negotiated between the parties involved.

Many agencies require, in writing, affiliation agreements (a mutual agreement to share services between agencies) and building space commitments prior to either grant approval or award. A useful method of generating community support may be to hold meetings with the top decision makers in the community who would be concerned with the subject matter of the proposal. The forum for discussion may include a query into the merits of the proposal, development of a contract of support for the proposal, to generate data in support of the proposal, or development of a strategy to create proposal support from a large number of community groups.

Identification of a Funding Resource

A review of the Objectives and Uses and Use Restrictions sections of the Catalog program description can point out which programs might provide funding for an idea. Do not overlook the related programs as potential resources. Both the applicant and the grantor agency should have the same interests, intentions, and needs if a proposal is to be considered an acceptable candidate for funding.

Once a potential grantor agency is identified, call the contact telephone number identified in Information Contacts and ask for a grant application kit. Later, get to know some of the grantor agency personnel. Ask for suggestions, criticisms, and advice about the proposed project. In many cases, the more agency personnel know about the proposal, the better the chance of support and of an eventual favorable decision. Sometimes it is useful to send the proposal summary to a specific agency official in a separate cover letter, and ask for review and comment at the earliest possible convenience. Always check with the Federal agency to determine its preference if this approach is under consideration. If the review is unfavorable and differences cannot be resolved, ask the examining agency (official) to suggest another department or agency which may be interested in the proposal. A personal visit to the agency's regional office or headquarters is also important. A visit not only establishes face-to-face contact, but also may bring out some essential details about the proposal or help secure literature and references from the agency's library.

Federal agencies are required to report funding information as funds are approved, increased or decreased among projects within a given State depending on the type of required reporting. Also, consider reviewing the Federal Budget for the current and budget fiscal years to determine proposed dollar amounts for particular budget functions.

The applicant should carefully study the eligibility requirements for each Federal program under consideration (see the Applicant Eligibility section of the Catalog program description). The applicant may learn that he or she is required to provide services otherwise unintended such as a service to particular client groups, or involvement of specific institutions. It may necessitate the modification of the original concept in order for the project to be eligible for funding. Questions about eligibility should be discussed with the appropriate program officer.

Deadlines for submitting applications are often not negotiable. They are usually associated with strict timetables for agency review. Some programs have more than one application deadline during the fiscal year. Applicants should plan proposal development around the established deadlines.

Getting Organized to Write the Proposal

Throughout the proposal writing stage keep a notebook handy to write down ideas. Periodically, try to connect ideas by reviewing the notebook. Never throw away written ideas during the grant writing stage. Maintain a file labeled "Ideas" or by some other convenient title and review the ideas from time to time. The file should be easily accessible. The gathering of documents such as articles of incorporation, tax exemption certificates, and bylaws should be completed, if possible, before the writing begins.

REVIEW

Criticism

At some point, perhaps after the first or second draft is completed, seek out a neutral third party to review the proposal working draft for continuity, clarity and reasoning. Ask for constructive criticism at this point, rather than wait for the Federal grantor agency to volunteer this information during the review cycle. For example, has the writer made unsupported assumptions or used jargon or excessive language in the proposal?

Signature

Most proposals are made to institutions rather than individuals. Often signatures of chief administrative officials are required. Check to make sure they are included in the proposal where appropriate.

Neatness

Proposals should be typed, collated, copied, and packaged correctly and neatly (according to agency instructions, if any). Each package should be inspected to ensure uniformity from cover to cover. Binding may require either clamps or hard covers. Check with the Federal agency to determine its preference. A neat, organized, and attractive proposal package can leave a positive impression with the reader about the proposal contents.

Mailing

A cover letter should always accompany a proposal. Standard U.S. Postal Service requirements apply unless otherwise indicated by the Federal agency. Make sure there is enough time for the proposals to reach their destinations. Otherwise, special arrangements may be necessary. Always coordinate such arrangements with the Federal grantor agency project office (the agency which will ultimately have the responsibility for the project), the grant office (the agency which will coordinate the grant review), and the contract office (the agency responsible for disbursement and grant award notices), if necessary.

WRITING THE GRANT PROPOSAL

The Basic Components of a Proposal

There are eight basic components to creating a solid proposal package: (1) the proposal summary; (2) introduction of organization; (3) the problem statement (or needs assessment); (4) project objectives; (5) project methods or design; (6) project evaluation; (7) future funding; and (8) the project budget. The following will provide an overview of these components.

The Proposal Summary: Outline of Project Goals

The proposal summary outlines the proposed project and should appear at the beginning of the proposal. It could be in the form of a cover letter or a separate page, but should definitely be brief -- no longer than two or three paragraphs. The summary would be most useful if it were prepared after the proposal has been developed in order to encompass all the key summary points necessary to communicate the objectives of the project. It is this document that becomes the cornerstone of your proposal, and the initial impression it gives will be critical to the success of your venture. In many cases, the summary will be the first part of the proposal package seen by agency officials and very possibly could be the only part of the package that is carefully reviewed before the decision is made to consider the project any further.

The applicant must select a fundable project which can be supported in view of the local need. Alternatives, in the absence of Federal support, should be pointed out. The influence of the project both during and after the project period should be explained. The consequences of the project as a result of funding should be highlighted.

Introduction: Presenting a Credible Applicant or Organization

The applicant should gather data about its organization from all available sources. Most proposals require a description of an applicant's organization to describe its past and present operations. Some features to consider are:

A brief biography of board members and key staff members.

The organization's goals, philosophy, track record with other grantors, and any success stories.

The data should be relevant to the goals of the Federal grantor agency and should establish the applicant's credibility.

The Problem Statement: Stating the Purpose at Hand

The problem statement (or needs assessment) is a key element of a proposal that makes a clear, concise, and well-supported statement of the problem to be addressed. The best way to collect information about the problem is to conduct and document both a formal and informal needs assessment for a program in the FF-4 11-08 target or service area. The information provided should be both factual and directly related to the problem addressed by the proposal. Areas to document are:

The purpose for developing the proposal.

The beneficiaries -- who are they and how will they benefit.

The social and economic costs to be affected.

The nature of the problem (provide as much hard evidence as possible).

How the applicant organization came to realize the problem exists, and what is currently being done about the problem.

The remaining alternatives available when funding has been exhausted. Explain what will happen to the project and the impending implications.

Most importantly, the specific manner through which problems might be solved. Review the resources needed, considering how they will be used and to what end.

There is a considerable body of literature on the exact assessment techniques to be used. Any local, regional, or State government planning office, or local university offering course work in planning and evaluation techniques should be able to provide excellent background references.

Types of data that may be collected include: historical, geographic, quantitative, factual, statistical, and philosophical information, as well as studies completed by colleges, and literature searches from public or university libraries. Local colleges or universities which have a department or section related to the proposal topic may help determine if there is interest in developing a student or faculty project to conduct a needs assessment. It may be helpful to include examples of the findings for highlighting in the proposal.

Project Objectives: Goals and Desired Outcome

Program objectives refer to specific activities in a proposal. It is necessary to identify all objectives related to the goals to be reached, and the methods to be employed to achieve the stated objectives. Consider quantities or things measurable and refer to a problem statement and the outcome of proposed activities when developing a well-stated objective. The figures used should be verifiable. Remember, if the proposal is funded, the stated objectives will probably be used to evaluate program progress, so be realistic. There is literature available to help identify and write program objectives.

Program Methods and Program Design: A Plan of Action

The program design refers to how the project is expected to work and solve the stated problem. Sketch out the following:

A flow chart of the organizational features of the project. Describe how the parts interrelate, where personnel will be needed, and what they are expected to do. Identify the kinds of facilities, transportation, and support services required (throughputs).

Explain what will be achieved through 1 and 2 above (outputs); i.e., plan for measurable results. Project staff may be required to produce evidence of program performance through an examination of stated objectives during either a site visit by the Federal grantor agency and or grant reviews which may involve peer review committees.

It may be useful to devise a diagram of the program design. For example, draw a three column block. Each column is headed by one of the parts (inputs, throughputs and outputs), and on the left 11-08 FF-5 (next to the first column) specific program features should be identified (i.e., implementation, staffing, procurement, and systems development). In the grid, specify something about the program design, for example, assume the first column is labeled inputs and the first row is labeled staff. On the grid one might specify under inputs five nurses to operate a child care unit. The throughput might be to maintain charts, counsel the children, and set up a daily routine; outputs might be to discharge 25 healthy children per week. This type of procedure will help to conceptualize both the scope and detail of the project.

Wherever possible, justify in the narrative the course of action taken. The most economical method should be used that does not compromise or sacrifice project quality. The financial expenses associated with performance of the project will later become points of negotiation with the Federal program staff. If everything is not carefully justified in writing in the proposal, after negotiation with the Federal grantor agencies, the approved project may resemble less of the original concept. Carefully consider the pressures of the proposed implementation, that is, the time and money needed to acquire each part of the plan. A Program Evaluation and Review Technique (PERT) chart could be useful and supportive in justifying some proposals.

The remaining alternatives available when funding has been exhausted. Explain what will happen to the project and the impending implications.

Highlight the innovative features of the proposal which could be considered distinct from other proposals under consideration.

Whenever possible, use appendices to provide details, supplementary data, references, and information requiring in-depth analysis. These types of data, although supportive of the proposal, if included in the body of the design, could detract from its readability. Appendices provide the proposal reader with immediate access to details if and when clarification of an idea, sequence or conclusion is required. Time tables, work plans, schedules, activities, methodologies, legal papers, personal vitae, letters of support, and endorsements are examples of appendices.

Evaluation: Product and Process Analysis

The evaluation component is two-fold: (1) product evaluation; and (2) process evaluation. Product evaluation addresses results that can be attributed to the project, as well as the extent to which the project has satisfied its desired objectives. Process evaluation addresses how the project was conducted, in terms of consistency with the stated plan of action and the effectiveness of the various activities within the plan.

Most Federal agencies now require some form of program evaluation among grantees. The requirements of the proposed project should be explored carefully. Evaluations may be conducted by an internal staff member, an evaluation firm or both. The applicant should state the amount of time needed to evaluate, how the feedback will be distributed among the proposed staff, and a schedule for review and comment for this type of communication. Evaluation designs may start at the beginning, middle or end of a project, but the applicant should specify a start-up time. It is practical to submit an evaluation design at the start of a project for two reasons:

Convincing evaluations require the collection of appropriate data before and during program operations; and,

If the evaluation design cannot be prepared at the outset then a critical review of the program design may be advisable.

Even if the evaluation design has to be revised as the project progresses, it is much easier and cheaper to modify a good design. If the problem is not well defined and carefully analyzed for cause and effect relationships then a good evaluation design may be difficult to achieve. Sometimes a pilot study is needed to begin the identification of facts and relationships. Often a thorough literature search may be sufficient.

Evaluation requires both coordination and agreement among program decision makers (if known). Above all, the Federal grantor agency's requirements should be highlighted in the evaluation design. Also, Federal grantor agencies may require specific evaluation techniques such as designated data formats (an existing FF-6 11-08 information collection system) or they may offer financial inducements for voluntary participation in a national evaluation study. The applicant should ask specifically about these points. Also, consult the Criteria For Selecting Proposals section of the Catalog program description to determine the exact evaluation methods to be required for the program if funded.

Future Funding: Long-Term Project Planning

Describe a plan for continuation beyond the grant period, and/or the availability of other resources necessary to implement the grant. Discuss maintenance and future program funding if program is for construction activity. Account for other needed expenditures if program includes purchase of equipment.

The Proposal Budget: Planning the Budget

Funding levels in Federal assistance programs change yearly. It is useful to review the appropriations over the past several years to try to project future funding levels (see Financial Information section of the Catalog program description).

However, it is safer to never anticipate that the income from the grant will be the sole support for the project. This consideration should be given to the overall budget requirements, and in particular, to budget line items most subject to inflationary pressures. Restraint is important in determining inflationary cost projections (avoid padding budget line items), but attempt to anticipate possible future increases.

Some vulnerable budget areas are: utilities, rental of buildings and equipment, salary increases, food, telephones, insurance, and transportation. Budget adjustments are sometimes made after the grant award, but this can be a lengthy process. Be certain that implementation, continuation and phase-down costs can be met. Consider costs associated with leases, evaluation systems, hard/soft match requirements, audits, development, implementation and maintenance of information and accounting systems, and other long-term financial commitments.

A well-prepared budget justifies all expenses and is consistent with the proposal narrative. Some areas in need of an evaluation for consistency are: (1) the salaries in the proposal in relation to those of the applicant organization should be similar; (2) if new staff persons are being hired, additional space and equipment should be considered, as necessary; (3) if the budget calls for an equipment purchase, it should be the type allowed by the grantor agency; (4) if additional space is rented, the increase in insurance should be supported; (5) if an indirect cost rate applies to the proposal, the division between direct and indirect costs should not be in conflict, and the aggregate budget totals should refer directly to the approved formula; and (6) if matching costs are required, the contributions to the matching fund should be taken out of the budget unless otherwise specified in the application instructions.

It is very important to become familiar with Government-wide circular requirements. The Catalog identifies in the program description section (as information is provided from the agencies) the particular circulars applicable to a Federal program, and summarizes coordination of Executive Order 12372, "Intergovernmental Review of Programs" requirements in Appendix I. The applicant should thoroughly review the appropriate circulars since they are essential in determining items such as cost principles and conforming with Government guidelines for Federal domestic assistance.

6. Special Bonus:

Sixty One Ways to Save Money

Here is a list of tips and ideas that will help you save money in various areas of your life:

Airline Fares

1.You may lower the price of a round trip air fare by as much as two-thirds by making certain your trip includes a Saturday evening stay over, and by purchasing the ticket in advance.

2.To make certain you have a cheap fare, even if you use a travel agent, contact all the airlines that fly where you want to go and ask what the lowest fare to your destination is.

3.Be flexible, if possible. Consider using low fare carriers or alternative airports and keep an eye out for fare wars.

Car Rental

1.Since car rental rates can vary greatly, shop around for the best basic rates. Ask about any additional charges (extra driver, gas, drop-off fees) and special offers.

2.Rental car companies offer various insurance and waiver options. Check with your automobile insurance agent and credit card company in advance to avoid duplicating any coverage you may already have.

New Cars

1.You can save thousands of dollars over the lifetime of a car by selecting a model that combines a low purchase price with low financing, insurance, gasoline, maintenance, and repair costs. Ask your local librarian for new car guides that contain this information.

2.Having selected a model, you can save hundreds of dollars by comparison shopping. Call at least five dealers for price quotes and let each know that you are calling others.

3.Remember there is no "cooling off" period on new car sales. Once you have signed a contract, you are obligated to buy the car.

Used Cars

1.Before buying any used car:

- Compare the seller's asking price with the average retail price in a "bluebook" or other guide to car prices found at many libraries, banks, and credit unions.

- Have a mechanic you trust check the car, especially if the car is sold "as is."

2.Consider purchasing a used car from an individual you know and trust. They are more likely than other sellers to charge a lower price and point out any problems with the car.

Auto Leasing

1.Don't decide to lease a car just because the payments are lower than on a traditional auto loan. The leasing payments may be lower because you don't own the car at the end of the lease.

2.Leasing a car is very complicated. When shopping, consider the price of the car (known as the capitalized cost), your trade-in allowance, any down payment, monthly payments, various fees (excess mileage, excess "wear and tear," end-of- lease), and the cost of buying the car at the end of the lease. Keys to Vehicle Leasing: A Consumer Guide, published by the Federal Reserve Board and Federal Trade Commission, is a valuable source of information about auto leasing.

Gasoline

1.You can save hundreds of dollars a year by comparing prices at different stations, pumping gas yourself, and using the lowest-octane called for in your owner's manual.

2.You can save up to $100 a year on gas by keeping your engine tuned and your tires inflated to their proper pressure.

Car Repairs

1.Consumers lose billions of dollars each year on unneeded

or poorly done car repairs. The most important step that you can take to save money on these repairs is to find a skilled, honest mechanic. Before you need repairs, look for a mechanic who:

- is certified and well established;

- has done good work for someone you know; and

- communicates well about repair options and costs.

Auto Insurance

1.You can save several hundred dollars a year by purchasing auto insurance from a licensed, low-price insurer. Call your state insurance department for a publication showing typical prices charged by different companies. Then call at least four of the lowest-priced, licensed insurers to learn what they would charge you for the same coverage.

2.Talk to your agent or insurer about raising your deductibles on collision and comprehensive coverages to at least $500 or, if you have an old car, dropping these coverages altogether. Taking these steps can save you hundreds of dollars a year.

3.Make certain that your new policy is in effect before dropping your old one.

Homeowner/Renter Insurance

1.You can save several hundred dollars a year on

homeowner insurance and up to $50 a year on renter insurance by purchasing insurance from a low-price, licensed insurer. Ask your state insurance department for a publication showing typical prices charged by different licensed companies. Then call at least four of the lowest priced insurers to learn what they would charge you. If such a publication is not available, it is even more important to call at least four insurers for price quotes.

2.Make certain you purchase enough coverage to replace the house and its contents. "Replacement" on the house means rebuilding to its current condition.

3.Make certain your new policy is in effect before dropping your old one.

Life Insurance

1.If you want insurance protection only, and not a savings and investment product, buy a term life insurance policy.

2.If you want to buy a whole life, universal life, or other cash value policy, plan to hold it for at least 15 years. Canceling these policies after only a few years can more than double your life insurance costs.

3.Check your public library for information about the financial soundness of insurance companies and the prices they charge. The July 1998 issue of Consumer Reports is a valuable source of information about a number of insurers.

Checking

1.You can save more than $100 a year in fees by selecting a checking account with a low (or no) minimum balance requirement that you can, and do, meet. Request a list of these and other fees that are charged on these accounts.

2.Banking institutions often will drop or lower checking fees if paychecks are directly deposited by your employer. Direct deposit offers the additional advantages of convenience, security, and immediate access to your money.

Savings and Investment Products

1.Before opening a savings or investment account with a bank or other financial institution, find out whether the account is insured by the federal government (FDIC or NCUA). An increasing number of products offered by these institutions, including mutual stock funds and annuities, are not insured.

2.To earn the highest return on savings (annual percentage yield) with little or no risk, consider certificates of deposit (CDs) and treasury bills or notes.

3.Once you select a type of savings or investment product, compare rates and fees offered by different institutions. These rates can vary a lot and, over time, can significantly affect interest earnings.

Credit Cards

1. You can save as much as a thousand dollars or more each year in lower credit card interest charges by paying off your entire bill each month.

2. If you are unable to pay off a large balance, pay as much as you can and switch to a credit card with a low annual percentage rate (APR). For a modest fee, RAM Research Corp. (800-344-7714) will send you a list of low-rate cards. You can obtain a list of low-rate cards by accessing "www.ramresearch.com.cardtrack" on the Internet.

3. You can reduce credit card fees, which may add up to more than $100 a year, by getting rid of all but one or two cards, and by avoiding late payment and over-the-credit limit fees.

Auto Loans

1. If you have significant savings earning a low interest rate, consider making a large down payment or even paying for the car in cash. This could save you as much as several thousand dollars in finance charges.

2. You can save as much as hundreds of dollars in finance charges by shopping for the cheapest loan. Contact several banks, your credit union, and the auto manufacturer's own finance company.

First Mortgage Loans

1. Although your monthly payment may be higher, you can

save tens of thousands of dollars in interest charges by shopping for the shortest-term mortgage you can afford. On a $100,000 fixed-rate loan at 8% annual percentage rate (APR), for example, you will pay $90,000 less in interest on a 1 5-year mortgage than on a 30-year mortgage.

2.You can save thousands of dollars in interest charges by shopping for the lowest-rate mortgage with the fewest points. On a 15-year, $100,000 fixed-rate mortgage, just lowering the APR from 8.5% to 8.0% can save you more than $5,000 in interest charges. On this mortgage, paying two points instead of three would save you an additional $1,000.

3.If your local newspaper does not periodically run mortgage rate surveys, call at least six lenders for information about their rates (APRs), points, and fees. Then ask an accountant to compute precisely how much each mortgage option will cost and its tax implications.

4.Be aware that the interest rate on most adjustable rate mortgage loans (ARMs) can vary a great deal over the lifetime of the mortgage. An increase of several percentage points might raise payments by hundreds of dollars per month.

Mortgage Refinancing

1.Consider refinancing your mortgage if you can get a rate that is at least one percentage point lower than your existing mortgage rate and plan to keep the new mortgage for several years or more. Ask an accountant to calculate precisely how much your new mortgage (including up-front fees) will cost and whether, in the long run, it will cost less than your current mortgage.

Home Equity Loans

1.Be cautious in taking out home equity loans. These loans reduce the equity that you have built up in your home. If you are unable to make payments, you could lose your home.

2.Compare home equity loans offered by at least four banking institutions. In comparing these loans, consider not only the annual percentage rate (APR) but also points, closing costs, other fees, and the index for any variable rate changes.

Home Purchase

1.You can often negotiate a lower sale price by employing a buyer broker who works for you not the seller. If the buyer broker or the broker's firm also lists properties, there may be a conflict of interest, so ask them to tell you if they are showing you a property that they have listed.

2.Do not purchase any house until it has been examined by a home inspector that you selected.

Renting a Place to Live

1.Do not limit your rental housing search to classified ads or referrals from friends and acquaintances. Select buildings where you would like to live and contact their building manager or owner to see if anything is available.

2.Remember that signing a lease probably obligates you to make all monthly payments for the term of the agreement.

Home Improvement

1.Home repairs often cost thousands of dollars and are the subject of frequent complaints. Select from among several well established, licensed contractors who have submitted written, fixed-price bids for the work.

2.Do not sign any contract that requires full payment before satisfactory completion of the work.

Major Appliances

1.Consult Consumer Reports, available in most public libraries, for information about specific brands and how to evaluate them, including energy use. There are often great price and quality differences among brands.

2.Once you've selected a brand, check the phone book to learn what stores carry this brand, then call at least four of these stores for the prices of specific models. After each store has given you a quote, ask if that's the lowest price they can offer you. This comparison shopping can save you as much as $100 or more.

Electricity

1.To save as much as hundreds of dollars a year on electricity, make certain that any new appliances you purchase, especially air conditioners and furnaces, are energy-efficient. Information on the energy efficiency of major appliances is found on Energy Guide Labels required by federal law.

2.Enrolling in load management programs and off-hour rate programs offered by your electric utility may save you up to $100 a year in electricity costs. Call your electric utility for information about these cost-saving programs.

Home Heating

1.A home energy audit can identify ways to save up to hundreds of dollars a year on home heating (and air conditioning). Ask your electric or gas utility if they can do this audit for free or for a reasonable charge. If they cannot, ask them to refer you to a qualified professional.

Local Telephone Service

1.Check with your phone company to see whether a flat rate or measured service plan will save you the most money.

2.You will usually save money by buying your phones instead of leasing them.

3.Check your local phone bill to see if you have optional services that you don't really need or use. Each option you drop could save you $40 or more each year.

Long Distance Telephone Service

1.Long distance calls made during evenings, at night, or on weekends can cost significantly less than weekday calls.

2.If you make more than a few long distance calls each month, consider subscribing to a calling plan. Call several long distance companies to see which one has the least expensive plan for the calls you make.

3.Whenever possible, dial your long distance calls directly. Using the operator to complete a call can cost you an extra $6.

Food Purchased at Markets

1.You can save hundreds of dollars a year by shopping at the lower-priced food stores. Convenience stores often charge the highest prices.

2.You will spend less on food if you shop with a list.

3.You can save hundreds of dollars a year by comparing price-per-ounce or other unit prices on shelf labels. Stock up on those items with low per-unit costs.

Prescription Drugs

1.Since brand name drugs are usually much more expensive than their generic equivalents, ask your physician and pharmacist for generic drugs whenever appropriate.

2.Since pharmacies may charge widely different prices for the same medicine, call several. When taking a drug for a long time, also consider calling mail-order pharmacies, which often charge lower prices.

Funeral Arrangements

1.Make your wishes known about your funeral, memorial, or burial arrangements in writing. Be cautious about prepaying because there may be risks involved.

2.For information about the least costly options, which could save you several thousand dollars, contact a local memorial society, which is usually listed in the Yellow Pages under funeral services.

3.Before selecting a funeral home, call several and ask for prices of specific goods and services, or visit them to obtain an itemized price list. You are entitled to this information by law and, by using it to comparison shop, you can save hundreds of dollars.